D1164468

R. T. STUMP

The

SIGN

of the

CROSS

A SERIES OF LENTEN SERMONS

BY

O. P. KRETZMANN

CONCORDIA PUBLISHING HOUSE
SAINT LOUIS, MISSOURI

The Library of Congress has cataloged this book as follows:

Kretzmann, Otto Paul, 1901—
    The sign of the cross, a series of Lenten sermons.
Saint Louis, Concordia Pub. House [ᶜ1959]

    86 p.   22 cm.

    1. Lenten sermons.   2. Lutheran Church — Sermons.
3. Sermons, American. I. Title.

BV4277.K7   252.6   59-6231 ‡

Library of Congress

Copyright 1959 by
Concordia Publishing House
Saint Louis, Missouri

MANUFACTURED IN THE UNITED STATES OF AMERICA

CONTENTS

The
SIGN
of
FORGIVENESS

Then said Jesus, Father, forgive them, for they know not what they do. And they parted His raiment and cast lots.   LUKE 23:34

One of the strange, mysterious marks of the church of the twentieth century is the fact that between Ash Wednesday and Easter Sunday morning there will be more people in the churches of Christendom than at any other time of the year. In order to understand this more clearly, it becomes necessary to examine these crowds more closely. Essentially there are three groups in our churches during the season of Lent. First, there are those who will be there also in July and August — the steady, quiet saints who are the glory of the kingdom of God on earth. Second, there are those who are in church during Lent by custom and tradition. They have learned from their childhood that this is a good time to be in church. Actually, it does not mean very much except that they catch a glimpse of the faith of their childhood. Third, there are those who are somehow haunted by the gallant figure of the lonely Sufferer on the cross. Their minds, cut by the acids of modernity, have succumbed to a vague, uneasy feeling that He knew something which life and time have taken away from the world. They see in Him a relentless strength, a far hope, and a continuing dream of goodness which the modern world has so largely forgotten.

All these people, however, have one purpose in common. They have come to see a man die. There is a strange fascination about this. Death is the one universal and inevitable experience. Further, the human race has discovered that we can learn how to live by practice. Each experience, whether it be happy or tragic, will, if we are wise, teach us something about the next. For the supreme experience of death, however, life furnishes no rehearsal. We can learn only by walking to the last door with others, by listening to their dying words and carrying them in re-membering hearts for the day when we, too, shall join the majority of the wise and the silent.

We, too, have come to this church to see a man die. Even humanly speaking, He is one of the great figures of life and history. Even the most hardened unbeliever will admit that He changed the course of history. His dying words, therefore, must be tremendously and enormously important.

Seven times He spoke, three times to men, three times to God, and once to Himself.

The first word from the cross — "Father, forgive them, for they know not what they do" — is totally unexpected. He says nothing about Himself. Like lightning our Lord's first words strike straight into the heart of all the tragedy of mankind. The face under the crown of thorns goes up. The marching years become the accompaniment of His words, and the crowd around the cross is transformed into the human race. The world hears a dying man point to the reason for death: "Father, forgive them, for they know not what they do."

Surely this is no sudden thought without a long background and without a profound cause. This word reaches far back beyond the centuries into the quiet unbroken calm of eternity, where there was only God. It reaches back into the counsels of the Holy Trinity, where there was the vision of the cross against the darkened sky and the far silhouette of those torn and lifeless

7

arms. It reaches back into the garden in the cool of the day when Adam and Eve were hiding from the voice of God after the fall into sin. It reaches back into all the voices of the prophets and kings who had said something about this dying Man on the cross. It reflects the quiet night when there was a Child born in a stable at Bethlehem. It reminds us of the words of our Apostolic Creed: "born of the Virgin Mary, suffered under Pontius Pilate, was crucified, dead, and buried."

This now was the fulfillment of all these events. It was Friday forenoon. A crowd poured out of the Damascus Gate. This was the climax of the drama of redemption. Now God could do no more. His infinite love for mankind was now reflected most clearly in the person, the work, and the words of His only-begotten Son dying on the cross. This first word is, therefore, for all our yesterdays and all our tomorrows. It is not only for those who are standing there but for all men who have lived and will live. It picks up all the years and rolls them up to heaven for the forgiveness of our heavenly Father.

There are few words in Holy Writ which more clearly point to the tremendous, dark, and tragic fact of sin. It is necessary for us today to stay with this thought for a moment. There are some things we can do about sin. We can be sorry for it. We can regret it. We can weep

8

over it. We can offer to make reparation when our sin has struck someone else. There is, however, one thing we cannot do about sin. We cannot forgive it. Someone has to go the long rest of the way. There must be a voice from the cross against the long silence of eternity, over the noise of two thousand years, "Father, forgive them, for they know not what they do."

"For they know not what they do!" We have all heard the agonized question: What is really wrong with the world and the human race? Here is the great answer: moral stupidity! There is a stupidity of the mind and a stupidity of the soul, and nothing in the world is more terribly fatal than the latter. After all, who crucified Jesus Christ? Men too blind to see who He was, too dull to hear the truth, too stupid to care about goodness and holiness and truth. How often has every faithful pastor heard the words, usually spoken in bitter tears: "If I had only known — what would happen with that careless word of mine, with my turning away from my friend, with my momentary anger or passion!" "If I had only known" — this is often the moral epitaph for a situation which can never be remedied by human thought or human effort.

And yet the tremendous, mysterious thing about this prayer is that it points to this moral stupidity as the basis for our Lord's plea for our forgiveness. "They know not what they do." They think that they are wise, intelligent, and shrewd — but, My heavenly Father, they are children. They are bad and wicked children. They do not know to what end their deeds finally lead. They do not have the imagination; they do not have the moral insight. Let it be said again, as it has been said these many hundreds of years, that sin is always unintelligent, stupid, and foolish. It always ends in the ashes of burned-out fires and the gray dust of shame.

All this is no faraway story or a lost and broken dream. This is the past, present, and future sign of the forgiveness of the Cross. Certainly all of us need this as we need nothing else. We have brought memories into this church of our own sins over the years. These memories burn. There are things that we should like to forget. The great, holy, and blessed thing about the sign of forgiveness is that a preacher can now stand up and under the Sign of the Cross give you this forgetfulness. There can be a drying of our tears over our sins. There can be relief from the tearing pain in our hearts. There can be a return to heaven and hope. "Father, forgive them, for they know not what they do." We may be children crying in the night, stupid, willful, and wrong, but we are still His children. By His grace we can now promise that we will try to do better.

10

We can come to His Cross in penitence and faith. If we do that, suddenly He is high and lifted up; and the age-old beautiful story of the Prodigal Son is re-enacted again and again in this church and all over the world.

When that happens by the grace and mercy of God, then there is also a second lesson we can learn from this word. Every day we pray: "Forgive us our trespasses as we forgive those who trespass against us." No amount of twisting and turning can get away from this fact: We are asking for forgiveness in the measure in which we are ready to forgive — no more and no less. We are tying our life to the life of God in Jesus Christ. It is therefore completely wrong to say, "I can forgive, but I cannot forget." By the grace of God we can do what God has done for us. We can also forget. He has forgotten our sins. He has buried them in the bottomless sea of His eternal pity. So we are to act in our realm, in our little life, as God acts in all life and history. Even though our time is so short and our way together so brief, we must find time to forgive and forget the trespasses and sins of others. There is no sense in staggering toward eternity with a heavy burden of grudges and hurts and jealousy and hate and malice. "Forgive us — as we forgive." This is one of the great signs of the Cross. This is God's way of doing things. It is the way of incredible power. It reflects a love that will not let go. It shows us again a love which bears all things for us.

Finally, there is no way in which the human heart can ignore this basic lesson of the Cross. It is true, of course, that sometimes men do not see the divine way — the way of forgiveness, of love and gentleness and humility. They feel that there are better ways of solving the deep and dark problems of the human heart. It is, therefore, necessary also for our generation to turn again and again to the Sign of the Cross. This way is always up. It leads finally beyond the flaming ramparts of our world to a world where there will at long last be no need of forgiveness and where we shall finally know, by His grace and mercy, what we are doing. We shall see very clearly that the ultimate power lies not in hate and fear and force but in forgiveness and love and grace. This is the Sign of the Cross.

The
SIGN
of
PEACE

Peace I leave with you, My peace I give unto you; not as the world giveth, give I unto you. Let not your heart be troubled, neither let it be afraid.   JOHN 14:27

About forty years have come and gone since America paused for a moment to bury in the National Cemetery at Arlington the body of the Unknown Soldier. Lost and forgotten in life, he was to become in death a perpetual symbol of the world's hope and a silent messenger of the world's peace. Near his tomb men placed an eternal light so that his memory might live in the grateful hearts of his countrymen. Today, forty years later, the dim and grim shadow of irony surrounds that light. Certainly we do not live in a world of peace. Today, forty years after the body of the Unknown Soldier found its last resting place, it looks as though he had died in vain. The world is haunted with fear, and the horizons of humanity are red with blood.

It is therefore vitally necessary for us to turn again and again to an old and yet ever new peace. It is interesting to note how often our Lord used that little word, how often it appears in the story of His visit with us from Bethlehem to the final hill in Galilee, how it rings like a tolling bell especially through His Maundy Thursday sermon and His high-priestly prayer. "Peace I leave with you" — this is finally the end of all He said and did for us. This is what He wanted us to have by His obedient life and atoning death.

Today we may well pause to inquire into the reasons for the world's loss of God's peace. Why do men hate one another? Why do the councils of the great of the earth calmly proceed to plan the killing of their fellow men? To answer these questions in terms of the demands for trade and territory, in terms of the personality of our leaders, in terms of the lust for power, does not strike at the heart of our problem. The answer is at the same time deeper and simpler than that! If you go out into nature at dusk, you will find that trees, stones, and hills cast shadows which are out of all proportion to the realities of the world and which will give you, if you attend only to them, a grotesque and utterly unreal picture of the realities behind these shadows. Something like that happens in the history of men with fearful regularity. Under the accumulated burden of fear upon fear and shame upon shame the eyes of men turn down and down and deeper down until they see only the shadows of the realities of God — the shadows which persuade them that momentary panaceas and temporary plans and endless conferences are going to heal the world's pain and turn away the world's ruin. There is no permanent hope in this. All the history of men and all the experience of the human heart are against it. You cannot heal a cancer by covering it with bandages. You cannot remove hate and fear and despair from the heart of the world by conducting some summit conferences. You may postpone their final result. But the realities are still here: the old envies, the old vanities, the old fears, the stark and grim reality of the sin-stricken heart of man — man who will hate and destroy and kill because there is no peace in his own heart.

Our Lord therefore speaks this Lenten season with particular force to the heart of the modern world: "Peace I leave with you, My peace I give unto you; not as the world giveth, give I unto you." There is the answer — the only answer which can stand up in the light of eternity. This is the peace which our Lord fills with a heavenly meaning. This is the peace which we can see in its full glory only under the shadow of the Cross to which we have brought our warring and restless hearts. This is the peace with God through the atonement of the Cross, peace wrought through the sanctifying power of God the Holy Spirit, peace in a world that is without peace.

This is the only answer to the world's problems which can stand up in the light of eternity. Today it is time for more of us to see it clearly before it is too late. Much has happened in the world since the Unknown Soldier was laid to rest. But nothing has come over our days and our years which would shake the deep and consuming conviction that today as seldom before the world must wait, not for the man of the hour or the program of the moment, but for the God of the eternities and the plan of the ages. We have looked around for help. Now it is time to look up. We have tried to plan a new world. Now it is time to plan a new life. We have asked ourselves what we want. Now it is time to ask what God wants. Far more than pacts and treaties we need today the new promise of an old peace — the voice of the Eternal pouring itself into the agony of life without God — the last hope of a generation driven to its knees by the overwhelming realization that

16

it has nowhere else to go: "Peace I leave with you, My peace I give unto you; not as the world giveth, give I unto you."

There it is! The peace of the Cross! Here is the profoundest need of our age. Often we may not be able to put it into words, but we know it in our hearts as we know nothing else. Some years ago Bertrand Russell summed it up in the following words: "Brief and powerless is man's life. On him and all his race the slow sure doom falls pitiless and dark. For him, condemned today to lose his dearest, tomorrow himself to pass through the gate of darkness, it remains only to cherish ere yet the blow falls the few hopes that ennoble his little life." I cannot see how men can live and die on that. There must be something which will make them glad and sure again, something to tell them that their brief mortal life has immortal meaning, something which will substitute for their deep dismay a peace and an understanding which the voices of despair and doubt can never give.

And the answer to this profound need lies in the simple words: "My peace I give unto you." On these words rests the last unity of the human heart which it, unaided and alone, can never know. This is the true peace of the child of God in the kingdom of God. Peace — the peace which the world cannot give, the peace which comes

17

from a surrendered happy faith in the atoning death of our Lord and Savior, the peace which passes the understanding of men, that comes and can come only from God. Long ago He gave it to the hearts of men through the obedient life and the atoning death of His only-begotten Son, Jesus Christ, our Lord. Through Him God spoke to the sin-stricken, hateful hearts of men finally and forever: "My peace I give unto you." Yesterday, today, and tomorrow this was, is, and shall be the peace which men need more bitterly than anything else — the peace of forgiven sin — the peace of a heart redeemed by the blood of the eternal Son of God — the peace which rests forever and ever in the sure knowledge that without the fear of any law or command our hearts rest quiet and still in the God-given spirit-filled faith which comes from the Prince of Peace. We cannot remove hate and blood and fear from the world while our hearts are at war with God. We cannot stand united in anything but the most transitory and fleeting concerns of our brief interlude between the eternities unless and until we stand united in the blessed unity of heaven, the majestic company of the redeemed of God, bound together by a common hope, a common love, and a common faith in Him who even today holds in His cross-torn hands the last peace of the human heart.

18

And this peace of the Cross is a very practical peace. While we may be concerned about the problems of the world — and God knows they are bad enough — we must be more immediately concerned about our own personal and individual problems. We cannot touch our world with the power of the conquering Christ unless we first look to ourselves, unless we view with deep concern any and all evidences which would rob us of the peace of the Cross. Among ourselves we must watch daily for anything that might destroy our deep essential unity in the Cross and leave us afraid and alone in this day of divine anger and winnowing. Our problem may be jealousy, envy, the love of material things, tiredness, restlessness — but whatever it may be, we must face it in the peace which comes from Christ and His Cross. We must hear His voice again above all our human weaknesses and failures, above our personal problems, above all that may stand in the way of our becoming better and greater inhabitants of His blessed kingdom. "Peace I leave with you, My peace I give unto you; not as the world giveth, give I unto you." Here is the last and ultimate hope of the human heart.

The
SIGN
of
UNDERSTANDING

And the Lord turned and looked upon Peter. And Peter remembered the word of the Lord, how He had said unto him, Before the cock crow thou shalt deny Me thrice.

And Peter went out and wept bitterly.

LUKE 22:61, 62

I wonder if you have felt the air of seeming unreality which surrounds the words of our text: "And the Lord turned and looked upon Peter. . . . And Peter went out and wept bitterly." This is one of the few silent moments in a night that was filled with shouting and lying and noise. One of the night's most significant events comes when two men suddenly look at each other. The hour was probably close to dawn. It was the end of a long and bitter night. Men were trying to get rid of their God.

Here there were now two men. One was only ten hours away from death. The other had just told a group of people around the fire that he did not know the Man who was going to His death. "No, no, I do not know Him. I have never been with Him. I swear I haven't."

And just then a cock crowed to greet the dawn. The Prisoner, apparently being led from one room of the palace to another, passed through the yard where the fire was. He looked at the man who stood there. Just a look! Suddenly the gate slammed, and out into the cold dawn fled the man who had been so loud and brave a moment earlier. He ran away and down the silent streets to hide himself in a corner of the great city; and as he ran, tears coursed down his face. They were hot and bitter tears, washing away something that was like dirt on his face and blood on his soul.

Certainly this is a strange scene. It is surely worth our time to examine it more closely. Just what happened there? I believe that the scene cannot be clear unless we understand that its meaning is far and deep and holy. Here at dawn, in one man looking at another, we catch a glimpse, revealing, terrifying, and healing, of the true meaning of the Christian faith.

Surely every thoughtful man or woman has

at times asked the question: Just what is this religion which has held the world for almost two thousand years and to which most of us give some form of allegiance? There is a picture of it here in the courtyard at dawn. In the long history of Christianity some men have said that the Christian religion is essentially a system of doctrine to be believed. If you know the doctrines and believe them, you are a Christian. This is, of course, partially true; but this alone would not explain the look which our Lord gave Peter or the resulting sudden tears.

There are others who have said Christianity is really a way of life. Until recent years this has been the great modern heresy, particularly in our own country. This, of course, is also partially true. Christianity is in one sense a way of life. But this definition, too, is far from complete. No, this scene, as few others in the sacred record, shows again that Christianity is basically and essentially a living relation to a living Person. It is always and forever the relationship of a redeemed human soul to the redeeming Person of Jesus Christ in faith, in love, in trust, in obedience, in all the ways in which one person is bound to another. This is really Christianity — nothing more and nothing less.

Now we can begin to understand what happened in the palace courtyard at dawn. As Peter was standing by the fire, lying for the sake of safety, swearing for a moment of warmth from the world's cold hate, he had broken that relationship to his Lord. He had thrown it away. He had turned against his Friend, his Savior, and his King. When his Savior turned and looked at Peter, he suddenly realized what he had done. He saw what he had thrown away and what he had forgotten. There was nothing to do but to stumble out into the dark, blinded by burning tears, afraid and alone, until another dawn a few weeks later when he would hear the voice of his Savior again, compelling, healing, and warm, by the lake: "Simon, son of Jonas, lovest thou Me?"

It is now time for us to bring this story down to the twentieth century as quickly as possible. Certainly all of us, if we are honest with ourselves and with God, will have to say: "I have done the same sort of thing. Perhaps I have not done it quite so obviously or so publicly, but there have been hours when I have forgotten. I have broken the bond between Jesus Christ and my soul. I, too, have stood by the sputtering little fires of my lusts, my greed, my hate, my tongue, my envy, my malice. I have acted as if I had never heard of Jesus Christ."

It is perfectly clear that a pattern for denial of Christ was set that night. A denial always has four parts. (1) It begins with a bad situation.

Peter should never have been standing by the fire. So also we, if we let ourselves in for situations which are made for a crack-up. (2) There comes the moment of forgetfulness. We want to be accepted by our environment. We want to be part of the crowd, no matter how bad and how evil it may be. (3) The break always comes. In our time and in our lives it is usually a denial by deed rather than by word. We do something which in its very nature is a denial of our Lord. (4) We can thank God that there is always the sign of understanding, the look of our Lord. Sometimes it is long in coming in the life of the individual. There may be years of seemingly getting by. But it is necessary that we mark it down: The look of our Lord always comes! He always turns around. Sometimes He looks at us in the still, small voice of our conscience, telling us that we did wrong. Sometimes He looks at nations in war and judgment. Sometimes He sees us in the voice of our pastor, the warning of a true friend, or a word from the Bible which suddenly strikes our mind and soul. He always turns around! He turns around to look at us and tell us that we are playing with life and with fire and dragging the sorrow of the ages across His soul, that we are breaking His heart and our own. If that realization leads to tears of regret and shame and repentance, then we, too, as Peter, are on the road to a new dawn, a voice tender, remembering, and forgiving: "My child, My child, lovest thou Me?"

It is vitally important for us to understand fully what His look can do. For this reason we ought to examine it very closely. What was there in the look of our Lord that brought Peter's world crashing about his ears and sent him out into the night in tears? Anger? No man who has merely been scolded has ever gone out into the night as Peter did. Reproach? Some, perhaps, but that was not all. The great, crushing power in that look, the elemental force which drove Peter into the night with heaven crying in his heart, the one thing that would remain with him in all the long and lonely years of wandering around the Mediterranean world, the one great power which would lift him, keep him, and drive him, was understanding love. This, then, is the sign of understanding and of love. It was only a glance, but in that glance were all the golden memories of blessed companionship and all the infinite and gentle tenderness of the immortal Shepherd for one sheep that had lost the way home. "And Peter went out and wept bitterly!" In heaven the recording angel wrote his name, indelibly and forever, among those whom love had brought home again. This is the Christian Gospel. This is the sign of understanding and forgiveness. This is all of it. In it is the greatness of our faith and the power of it! This is the Gospel of another chance. This is the haunting, eternal voice of our Savior: "I have loved thee with an everlasting love."

There is an old tradition in the Christian Church that this story has a very happy ending. It may be true, or it may be completely legendary, but it is singularly significant, with a certain justice and poetic fitness. It reports that on July 19, in the year of our Lord 64, thirty years after this night, a fire broke out in Rome. Half the city was destroyed. The Emperor Nero needed a scapegoat, and the Christians were at hand. According to the legend hundreds died by fire and the sword. Among them, according to the legend, was also Peter. At his own request he was crucified head downward because he did not consider himself worthy of dying in the same manner as his Lord had died. Here, then, the story ends. On a hot July morning an old man is hanging upside down in a Roman arena. If he opened his eyes, he saw the bloody red sand from which the church would grow in the years to come. But if he closed them, as I am sure he did — if he closed them in the moment of awareness and remembering of all the years that always comes to dying men — he saw something else. He saw many things in his own life, but surely above all, the dawn when he had looked into two eyes that understood him and loved him forever. He remembered the power that drove him out into the night to come at long last to this ridiculous position with the world upside down and tears of pain in his eyes once again. But now there was something else! He was waiting now for the moment when his Lord would come again to tell him that he had done well since that night, so well indeed that now the angels were waiting for him. He had kept the faith. And he knew, as he knew also that dawn by the lake, that now there would be no more night and no more tears. He was, I am sure, very content and very happy.

The
SIGN
of
AGONY

And being in an agony, He prayed more earnestly; and His sweat was as it were great drops of blood falling down to the ground. LUKE 22:44

All of us have learned how difficult it is to understand fully the sorrow and suffering of another person. To go beyond understanding to feeling is even more difficult. When tragedy strikes a friend, we can and should be sympathetic. We should suffer with him. However, we have also learned that no matter how hard we may try we can really never enter the inner recesses of the heart of another. This is where the last and deepest suffering takes place. Some time ago many newspapers reported the story of a little

28

child who was run over by a truck driven by a friend of the boy's family. Anyone who read the story was deeply shocked. Hearts went out to the parents and to the neighbor who was so innocently the cause of the tragedy. Many expressed their sympathy. And yet the last measure of suffering and sorrow was beyond the reach of our words. We were not able to cross the final barrier between their lives and ours.

Of course, God could enter into this sorrow — right into the very heart of it — but not we. There are always inner recesses and corners of the human personality which another person cannot reach. It is inevitably and tragically true that the ultimate sorrow of the human heart and soul must be borne alone. I am certain you will understand why I mention this. The task we have set for ourselves in our Lenten worship tonight is even more difficult. We must try to understand as clearly as we possibly can the suffering of a Man, not in our own community but in a garden six thousand miles away in space and two thousand years away in time.

Furthermore, this suffering Man was not only man but also God. We must understand His suffering not only with our minds but with our hearts. We must really sympathize with — "suffer with" — at least a part of His sorrow. Some of

29

His sorrow must become our sorrow, and some of His pain our pain.

Now one may legitimately ask the question: Why must we do this? There is only one answer. The suffering Man in the garden was and is our Savior. All of us were in His heart that night and that in a way which we can never fully understand on this side of the veil. We were a part of the agony of Gethsemane. The sin which we committed so easily and so carelessly yesterday or today was in that garden. It was the basic, ultimate, and terrible reason for the drops of blood, the sword in His heart, and the agony of His soul. The words of the great spiritual "Were You There When They Crucified My Lord?" also apply to Gethsemane. They come to us, even after all these years, with an insistent and powerful urgency. We were there.

There is, therefore, every reason for us to look very closely at the scene in the garden. Just what was going on there? What does it mean for our life and for our destiny?

Certainly it was a very strange situation. From time immemorial men had dreamed of God and the gods and of their meeting with divinity. They had built altars and temples for their deities. They had imagined the gods seated on Mount Olympus, or elsewhere, forever young, forever fair, aloof and cold. The gods were interested in men, but only to see to it that their laws were carried out and that transgressions of the laws of the universe were properly and inevitably punished. Gods were gods, and men were men. This was the way men thought the universe was arranged — before Bethlehem and Calvary.

Here now in Gethsemane, however, there is something amazingly different. Jesus Christ, God and man in one person, lies on His face beneath the olive trees. His sweat falls like drops of blood upon the earth. The immeasurable space around Him is filled with wheeling suns and stars which He has placed in the long whirling of the worlds. His hands — the same hands which were active at the creation of the universe — clutched the dust of the garden in agony. The Paschal moon — His moon — shines over waste oceans and waving treetops and looks down to light His face torn by an agony which was new on the earth.

Certainly there had never been anything like this in the long and bitter story of man. It may be that for some of us in this church now there will be in the years ahead some dark valleys, some agony of soul, some great loneliness. But we shall never know anything like this: all the world's aching sadness, this drying up of the fountains of life, this unimaginable sickening of soul. This was God and man suffering, and God can suffer more than men.

31

With this statement we are now beginning to touch the meaning of the scene, the reason for it, and the purpose of it. Perhaps there should be a warning at this point that many people will not want to see the true meaning of this agony under the Paschal moon. There may be various reasons for this reluctance to get close to it. Primarily, however, the reason lies in the fact that the true meaning of the agony in the garden is intimately, terribly, and eternally personal. It strikes every human being that has ever lived. It concerns every one of us in this church — and certainly we do not like to be directly involved in such terror of soul.

But there are also other human approaches to this agony. In order to soften the horror of the garden, men have said that His courage failed Him momentarily. He knew that in another twelve hours He would be dying on a cross. He was, they say, afraid of death. He did not want to go through with the next fifteen hours. This is obviously untrue. Could He have been afraid of death? Then He would have been weaker than many brave men who faced death without flinching. He would have been weaker than Stephen, whose face shone as the stones struck him. He would have been weaker than all the great company of martyrs, who met death gladly for His sake. He would have been even weaker than some of the men in this church tonight who looked squarely at death on the land, on the sea, and in the air during the days of war fifteen years ago.

No, it was nothing like that. He was not afraid of death or dying. If we look closely at His prayer in the garden, we see that He speaks to His Father not about tomorrow or what would happen on Friday afternoon. He is in agony over something that is happening right now. "This hour" — "this cup!" He is asking His Father in heaven to help Him in the climax of the atoning life and work which would go on until Friday afternoon. His agony of body and mind and soul was over something that struck Him under the olive trees with the disciples sleeping, the world at silent midnight, and the uncalled legions of angels looking on in horrified wonder. What was the real cause of His agony?

Anyone who is called to preach during Lent in the year of our Lord 1959 must say it very simply and clearly, again and again. It is the old, old story of sin and grace. What struck Him in the garden, pierced His soul, and painted incredible agony on His face was *sin*. There were voices, far and unheard, in the garden that night: "God hath made Him to be sin for us." "The Lord hath laid on Him the iniquity of us all." "Behold the Lamb of God, which taketh away the sin of the world." In some mysterious way known only to

33

God, all the timeless sin and sorrow of all life and history gathered in His soul that night in the garden. All of it was there. None of it was missing. He bore it all, and He bore it alone. No one was with Him in the wine press of divine judgment.

Now we must again make this very personal and very up to date. That bit of gossip in which we indulged a few days ago; that lingering impurity in our lives; that murder in the newspapers of our great cities; the hate in our hearts; these massacres in the concentration camps and prisons of our world — all of these, all of these were on His head that night. He was sin! He was sin and evil incarnate during that hour.

And having said that, we still shall never really know what it fully means, because it was one of the great unique experiences of the God-man. It is the heart of our entire Christian faith — the total transfer of sin to the bleeding head in the garden and on the cross.

There is, however, one way in which we can understand it. We may never fully grasp its meaning for *Him*, but its meaning for us is perfectly clear. We can leave this church today quiet, free, and forgiven by faith in His atoning suffering as our Substitute. Our faces can now be calm and peaceful because His face was torn by agony. We can look up to God because He looked down into the lowest corners of hell. Every evil thing

34

that worries us, every hidden sin, every fault we can leave in the garden with Him. He took care of it. It is His and no longer ours. This, you will understand, is the Christian religion — the religion of atonement, of redemption and forgiveness. And there is nothing else like it under the sun!

Perhaps there is one more thing that we should take from this service today. We should carry with us, too, the high and firm resolve to do a little better in the future than we have in the past. Pascal once said: "Jesus Christ is in agony until the end of the world." Upton Sinclair once wrote that one of the greatest causes of Jesus' suffering in the garden was the vision of what some of His faithless children would do to Him in all the years to come. And so today His agony is heard in all the sins of our time, in our carelessness with God and the suffering of all the images of God throughout the world. There is no greater way to live than to hear in all the pain and agony and horror of our time the echo of His agony, to resolve to help wherever we can, and to hear above the roar and confusion of our mad world His voice again and again: "Fear not, My child, I have already traveled that road. On each step of the terrible way I have left for you a drop of My blood and the print of My eternal mercy. Come in repentance and faith to Me, My lost and lonely child, and the way will always be clear and straight and bright for you." There is nothing greater and nothing more that you can possibly ask of God and His Son Jesus Christ, our suffering Lord. The Cross is now, and always, the sign of His agony for us and the sign of our joy in Him and our salvation.

The
SIGN
of
DECISION

But the chief priests and elders persuaded the multitude that they should ask Barabbas and destroy Jesus.

The governor answered and said unto them, Whether of the twain will ye that I release unto you? They said, Barabbas.

Pilate saith unto them, What shall I do then with Jesus, which is called Christ? They all say unto him, Let Him be crucified. MATT. 27:20-22

As we go through life we find that there are many difficult lessons which we must learn. There are the lessons of sorrow, of pain, of joy, of discipline, of patience, of waiting on God to work out His purposes in our lives. Perhaps no lesson, however, is more difficult than the slowly growing awareness of the fact that God does not always work at the same speed. Sometimes for years in our own life and for centuries in the lives of nations nothing much happens. Life is smooth, quiet, and uneventful. Time is a slow river moving imperceptibly to the sea. There is a deceptive stillness about life and time which can easily lull us into a false sense of security. And then suddenly things begin to move, the clocks of the world and of life strike together, the river of time roars with confusion, and the chariots of the living God sweep through life and the universe. The God of life and history and redemption swings into visible and evident action. "Hour of Decision

This is exactly what happened on that first Good — and evil — Friday almost two thousand years ago. Many years ago an instructor in English asked his class: "What is the greatest single dramatic scene in all the world's literature?" The members of the class immediately offered some suggestions. Some mentioned the opening scene of *Hamlet* at midnight on the platform at Elsinore. Others referred to the death of King Lear in the storm, the murder of Duncan in *Macbeth,* or the knocking on the door in the stricken silence after the murder. The slamming of the door by Nora in the final scene of Ibsen's *Doll House* was mentioned. In Holy Writ itself the scene in the eighth

38

chapter of the Gospel according to St. John between our Lord and the woman taken in adultery was cited. Finally the instructor said: "The greatest dramatic scenes in the entire world's literature are those which took place between six and nine o'clock on Good Friday morning."

This is probably true. Everything thinkable and unthinkable was going on. Every human passion was there: hate, anger, fear, love, pride, devotion. All the material of high drama was there: two trials, one murder, one suicide. There was always the tense waiting for the end.

It is a very curious drama too. It is held together only by the silent, mysterious figure of the leading Character, who speaks no more than one hundred words but who dominates the story as though He had rehearsed it from eternity. Here was God really moving fast, and when He moves, life and history and men move with Him to new, strange, but divinely appointed ends. He never moves alone.

Now we would like to present for your meditation the great final turning point in this drama. We have now reached the point of no return. It is the moment when it becomes finally clear that the drama can end in only one way. This is the final slamming of the door! It is the moment which takes us out of our seats as spectators and makes us participants in the drama. We are in it now for all time and all eternity.

Let us look more closely at the scene before us. From the very beginning of the drama the heart of the action lies in the decision made by those who come face to face with the silent figure of the thorn-crowned Sufferer, our Lord and Savior Jesus Christ. To their dismay they find that they cannot remain neutral. They must make up their minds about Him. The hour of decision has come. And so one by one, with a weird consistency, they make up their minds about what they are going to do with their God on a quiet morning in spring. Judas decides — and commits suicide. Peter decides — and stumbles off the stage with blinding tears in his eyes. Annas and Caiaphas decide — and get a few more years of shoddy, uneasy power. The disciples decide — and flee into a night without stars. The stage empties faster and faster until now, at the moment which we are considering, this moment of turning, there are only four characters left — a Roman, a criminal, a faceless mob, and the silent, strange, leading figure of Jesus Christ.

Curiously enough, the one man who has the hardest time making up his mind about Christ is not one of the disciples, but Pontius Pilate, the proud representative of a proud civilization. There are things inside him which seem to hold

40

him back. He has a sense of fairness, of Roman justice, of patrician contempt for these quarreling people. On the other hand, he is a twentieth-century man. He has power, and he means to keep it. And so he twists and turns. He talks and temporizes in the vain hope that he may find some way to get off the hook, to avoid a decision, to discover some way out of the dilemma. He would like to find some way of getting rid of his God standing there in the morning sunlight, the living embodiment of another world.

Finally in his desperation he hits upon a seemingly brilliant idea. He does not want to decide, so, even as you and I, he will try to let someone else do it. Let the people decide! He resolves to be democratic about the situation and give them the choice between good and evil, between God and man, between Jesus and Barabbas. He appeals to the group morality involved in the problem. Surely they will decide the right way! Has not someone said that the voice of the people is the voice of God? Are not many minds better than one? Is there not something good, something fundamentally sound in the common man which inevitably and invariably rises to the challenge of goodness? We can almost see his mind at work. Surely the people will recognize the thorn-crowned Sufferer as one of their own, their Friend, their Teacher, the carpenter's son from Nazareth.

Surely they will prefer Him to a murderer, a wild-eyed revolutionary, one of the anonymous criminals who were forever cluttering up the Roman jails all over the world. Surely this was an easy choice for the people! It was all so very clear and so very simple!

Today we all know what happened. Pilate asked his question — there was a roar from the crowd — and the noise of it was like the crack of doom in Pilate's ear: "Barabbas! Give us Barabbas!" The people had spoken. The election was over. The votes were in. The votes were counted, in earth and heaven and hell, finally and forever.

With this moment the scene becomes fearfully modern and contemporary. We may call this what we please — spiritual blindness, mob spirit, moral insanity. We may refer to our texts on psychology and sociology in order to explain just what happened here. We must never forget, however, that this was a cross section of our common humanity. These were people even as you and I. They were men and women from the homes, the shops, and the markets of Jerusalem. Here were students from the school of Gamaliel, good people, religious people — people who would not think of killing an animal on Saturday, but who are ready to kill their God on Friday. We are reminded of the end of a great Spanish

42

novel, *Blood and Sand,* in which the matador is dying and finally says, "I hear the roar of the only beast there is — humanity."

All this makes this scene very personal in its meaning for every one of us. Each of us in his own way must be a student of human nature. This is vital for a happy life. We must learn to get along with others. We want to know why people act as they do. Here — right here and now — is one of the great laboratories for such a study. Just why did the mob yell: "Barabbas! Give us Barabbas!"? Surely it was not because they hated our Lord Christ personally. Their leaders may have hated Him, but not the people themselves. He had come, as He had told them, to bring the Gospel to the poor, to bind up the brokenhearted, to tell captive souls that they were free, to open the eyes of the blind, to heal those that had been hurt and broken by life. My soul, you cannot hate anyone for that! No, we must understand clearly that there was something hopeless here, something deep and dark and demonic, something which you and I must face honestly if we are ever to understand human nature, life, and history. Here was something awful to see but necessary to understand. The people made their decision and cried "Barabbas," the world today cries "Barabbas," we cry "Barabbas," because they, the world, and we are under the deep, dark, demonic compulsion of sin. Here it is. All of it! It is clear and sharp in the morning sun. What was behind that cry on Friday morning is still behind it today. Sin! Cruelty, blasphemy, blind hate! All the whole vile catalog down to the last dregs of the lowest degeneracy. Every wrong appetite, every evil desire, every unnamed vice to the very last and the lowest of them all. Every sin of the world and in the world was there that morning. The sin of the past and the future, today's sin and yesterday's sin — this was behind the choice of the people. What was in the air that spring morning and is in the air in our own world is dark and evil. And so they cried "Barabbas!" James Russell Lowell tells of a painting in Brussels in which God is about to create the world and an angel is holding His arm: "If about to create such a world, stay Thy hand!" No, that is not the answer. It would be easy if we could blame all this on God, but God did not create a world of sin. This is our own doing. We can never blame anyone else for that.

Now, up to this point it is probably true that almost every realistic observer of the modern world would agree with what has been said. There seems to be no other way to explain what has happened to us, the way we dance and laugh on the edge of destruction, the seeming helplessness of the church, the dark, blind selfishness of men and nations. How can we explain this? All realistic observers will agree that it must be something like sin. There must be something really wrong with the very heart and soul of man. There must be something evil at the very core of human life, something which compels man to choose evil instead of God, which drives him to choose Barabbas again and again. In our time he usually chooses his own private, proud Barabbas, whoever or whatever he may be, just so long as he is a substitute for the living, redeeming God.

Concerning this many of us will agree. Now for the remainder of the truth which we confront today there will not be such universal agreement, perhaps not even in this church. It is now necessary for the preacher to present God's side of the story, a view that we can accept only by faith. It is at one and the same time simple and mysterious. If we in realism and penitence must identify ourselves with the people, God in His pity and grace identifies us with Barabbas, for whom our Lord became the Substitute, who went free because God was captive on a cross, who lived because Christ died. Now we are almost at the end of the story. This is what the theologian calls the mystery and miracle of grace. It always begins with a conversation between God and man. The conversation goes something like this:

Man, beaten and crushed: "I am a man of unclean life."

God: "I have redeemed thee, thou art Mine."

Man: "God, be merciful to me, a sinner."

God: "Rise, stand upon thy feet, and I will speak unto thee."

Here, then, the final, great eternal miracle happens again. Man stands up free and forgiven because one day there was a cross and his sin entered into the life and heart of the eternal Son of God made man. It was shared by God. It was buried in God. And because this great decision was made by God, we can leave this church today heads up, free and forgiven. We will go out again into a world engaged in a gigantic, terrifying conspiracy of defeat. In his *Farewell to Arms* Ernest Hemingway makes the modern temper articulate: "The world breaks everyone, and afterward many are strong at the broken places. But those that will not break it kills either swiftly or by slow torture. It kills the very gentle and the very brave impartially. If you are none of these, you can be sure it will kill you, too, but there will be no special hurry." This is the approach of many modern minds to life itself. This is the hopelessness and helplessness of many of our contemporaries. We know that we cannot possibly live on this. We can live only when we know that God has mended the broken places and that we are strong and free where He has come. We are free and forgiven by the great decision which He has made by the might and measure of the glory of the Cross.

Years ago a crowd was standing in a great square in London listening to the bell toll for the dead on Armistice Day. A man was standing in the crowd with his head bowed in prayer. A stranger spoke to him: "Do you really believe that these men are alive, that they are with God?" The man answered, "Yes." The stranger replied, "Yours must be a wonderful religion!" It is! It really is! When we know this, we are strong and safe in the full forgiveness of God for time and for eternity. God has made His decision, and by His grace we have made ours. And we have really made the right choice!

The
SIGN
of
MYSTERY

And when they were come to the place
which is called Calvary, there they crucified Him
and the malefactors, one on the right hand and
the other on the left. LUKE 23:33

It was nine o'clock on Good Friday morning.
It was probably a fair and warm spring morning
when the procession finally reached Calvary. Perhaps a little rain had fallen during the night, as it
does so often in the Holy Land at that season of
the year. The doves were circling above the hill.
The birds sang in the olive trees beneath the city
wall. It was a beautiful morning, a day for joy
and hope. It was an unusually good Friday.

I am certain that our Lord saw all that. He

48

who had watched the lilies of the field, the corn ripening for harvest, the moon standing above the valley of the Kidron — He would surely see once more the world as God had made it, beautiful and fair, a world of song and joy and hope, a world so far removed from the pain and tears and blood and hate with which the procession came to the little green hill beyond the gates of the Holy City.

And they crucified Him there! He was surrounded once more by the strange continuing goodness of all His creation except its crown, the body and soul of man, to which evil had come. The rest of creation was so beautiful and fair, but the heart of man was black with evil and sin.

They began to dig the hole for the cross. The crosspieces were fitted. His young body was laid on the beams. One nail was hammered home, then the second and the third. His arms and feet were bound tight with ropes because the nails might not hold the body racked with pain. Soldiers raised the cross upright. There was a dull thud as it fell into the hole dug for it. His blood started to flow from hands and feet. The aching, tearing pain of crucifixion began. They crucified Him there!

If we are really to see the meaning of the Cross, we must now go to Calvary and stand there with Him. This will be very good for us. We must stand there, not as contemporaries, because it

49

would be too easy for us to join the mob; we must stand there today as twentieth-century men and women, the seventieth generation since that first Good Friday. We stand there as the end products of 1,900 years of Christianity. We must stand at the edge of the crowd for a few moments and look very closely at the scene before us. Such an experience ought to be very much worthwhile, perhaps eternally decisive and everlastingly worthwhile.

Ever since Calvary there have been thousands of people in the world who have tried to make Christianity reasonable. Countless books have been written on the evidences of Christianity. They have been designed to prove that, after all, Christianity is a very reasonable thing, that you can think it through, that it appeals to the processes of thought and logic, the canons of human knowledge. Perhaps we should say again that much of this is very dangerous nonsense. The Christian religion is not a reasonable religion in the normal sense of the word. It is true, of course, that we can move around inside it by intellectual processes. We can formulate doctrines which are an exact reflection of the teachings of Holy Writ. We can reason from one proposition to another as theologians have done. We can work out conclusions on the basis of the inspired Word of God.

It must be said, however, that the great basic

truths are always and forever beyond reason. We cannot prove them by the ordinary laws of thought. As we examine our Christian faith, we go farther and farther until ultimately we always come to a jumping-off place. We arrive at the place where reason ends. We come to the place where we stand either with folded hands or with hands holding a hammer. We stand in the place from which we must leap into the arms of God if we want to be Christians. Calvary is always a place of mystery and of wonder. It is the final, burning focal point of the strange heavenly ways of God with men. This we must always remember as we come to the Cross ourselves or when we try to bring others into its healing shadow.

Here, where we are now standing on the edge of the crowd at Calvary, is the ultimate mystery — the mystery of the Cross. This is the riddle of God which can be solved only by God and in God and through His holy Word. We should freely admit that this just does not make sense in the way in which human beings interpret it. It is not reasonable — this cross, this mob, and God hanging there in the cool of a spring morning! As we stand there, the first question that comes to us is: What is behind all this? How did it happen?

The answer comes from faith, not from reason. We are face to face, as nowhere else in time and history, with the mystery of the evil in man.

51

The last, dark, bitter mystery of sin! Many centuries ago St. Anselm said to a young man who had his doubts and misgivings about the Christian Gospel: "You have not yet considered the seriousness of sin." It is true, of course, that our modern minds do not like this very much. We feel that, by and large, we are fairly good people. Our friends are fairly good people. People of other races and nations may sometimes be bad, but not we ourselves. Or if we are unusually intelligent, we go beyond this to say that the notion of man's essential sinfulness is unhistorical and unscientific. We must throw off this burden on man which has filled him with such a sense of guilt. We must now be ready to go forward to a religion of humanity. We must trust in the essential goodness of mankind. We must believe in our power to remake our environment. We must try to lift ourselves by our bootstraps into a new and better world.

No man can stand at the foot of the Cross and believe in these notions. Here we are face to face with the mystery of sin. This is not a crowd of unreasonable, thoughtless men. This is a mob of bad men, evil men, who have come to crucify their God. The young man hanging on the cross is 33 years old. He had committed no crime. For three years He had been engaged in a tremendous mission of healing and love. He had gone about doing good. And yet they were now killing Him!

The last thing He sees of humanity before He dies is a mob of grinning faces. The last thing He hears is a curse. The last thing He knows is hate and pain. Now, all this does not square for one moment with our theories of progress, our shallow belief in the essential goodness of humanity, and our false and fatal optimism concerning the destiny of the human race without God.

And so we turn again and again to our Bibles. There we find the answer to the mystery. We begin to believe and to understand the deep, dark problems which come to a climax at the cross. We find something which fits into our world and makes it much more understandable. We discover that sin is always hate. It is hate of God and man. It is the breaking down of all friendship and all fellowship between heaven and earth. It is the separation of God from man and man from man. We discover now the reason for the cross. It is the end of our long separation, our loneliness, our wandering, and our transgression. We had a love once, and we threw it out the window of our broken lives. We had a home once, and we turned away from it in hate and sin. We had a Friend once, and we left Him to die on the cross. The cross is only the last and ultimate expression of the dark terror in our souls, the bitterness of our lives, and all the brutality and tyranny

53

and injustice and greed which has piled up since Paradise Lost.

Having looked to the darkness of sin, we now turn back to the Cross to see some light in our darkness. Things become clearer. We begin to understand this ultimate mystery. It may be that we cannot understand everything, but we are beginning to find an answer to the question: Why is that young man hanging there? By His grace we know that He is God. Since He is God, where are the legions of angels? What keeps Him on the wooden bed of pain? Three nails? Those slivers of metal forged by human hands cannot possibly pin down God. There must be something else which holds Him to His dying! We have seen from Holy Writ the mystery of man and the mystery of sin. We are now face to face with the mystery of God. Our Lord Jesus Christ, the Savior of the world, is there on the cross because He wants to be there. He had wanted to hang there from the foundation of the earth, and He still wants to. It is neither the nails nor the new ropes that hold Him to His dying. It is just love and nothing else! It is the perfect love of the perfect God and the perfect love of a perfect man. Here we are face to face with the friendship of God pouring itself down and away through the cross. This is the miracle and the mystery of forgiveness. It is the restoration of fellowship with God and with man.

We lost a friend, and He came back to us. We lost a love, and He gave it back to us. We lost a home, and He brought it back to the dust where we must live.

The mystery now comes a little closer to our human understanding. It is still a mystery, as everything about God is, but we can see that it is and why it is. It is all strangely simple with the profound simplicity of God.

There are men who say that Christianity is a very complex thing. They report that they find it difficult to find their way through its message. We, however, can never forget that all of it is in two sentences and that all of it is terribly personal. There is, first, always the cry of the defeated soul: "God be merciful to me, a miserable sinner." Then there is always the answering cry of the young Man on the cross, our Lord and Savior, "Father, forgive them, for they know not what they do." This is the whole story. Christianity is always the story of people who have come back again. David crying in the night, Peter stumbling into the dark in tears, Paul on the road to Damascus! Always and forever they dash the tears from their eyes because now they see life and time and sin and death and hate and pain with the eyes of Him who looked at us from the cross, saw us as we were and are, and loved us nevertheless.

"While we were yet sinners" God, through His only-begotten Son, gave us life and peace.

Now for a moment we ought to leave Calvary and bring all that we have learned down to our own time and life. There is one more mystery about the Sign of the Cross. If we look hard at the world and history, we see its strange continuing power. This power needs more emphasis in our day, especially among those who have felt that the Christian Gospel is helpless over against the evil might of man. Too often we followers of our Lord Jesus Christ believe the Gospel, but we do not believe it hard enough. We approach it somewhat apologetically, and we bring it to men and women in the same way. Our attitude is much the same as the attitude of the pagan who said to his god, "Between us, I suspect that you do not exist." Our religion must be like an alpenstock which is so firm and sure and strong that it cannot be broken. We must have a faith which can stand up and take it! This means that we must stand at Calvary again and again in order to see the tremendous power of the love and mercy which broke the dominion of sin and gave us life and freedom and forgiveness.

To see this clearly is our task and our destiny, especially as twentieth-century Christians. To the seeing eye of faith the Cross today is no longer a mystery. It is the strong power which stands alone above the fallen of the earth. It is the power of Him in whose eyes the past and the future are the eternal Now. It is the power of Him who knows us even after all these years — us who own Him as King and Lord and who walk with Him through tears and tribulation and trial and time to the ultimate destiny of grace which He has laid up in heaven for us. It is the continuing power of Him who will come at last, not to a cross but to a throne. If we become His children, we have in Him, and in Him alone, the kingdom and the power and the glory forever and ever.

The
SIGN
of
POWER

And Jesus came and spake unto them, saying, All power is given unto Me in heaven and in earth. MATTHEW 28:18

At first glance this would appear to be a strange text for a Lenten sermon. These are words spoken by our Lord several weeks after the darkness of Maundy Thursday and Good Friday. And yet, just because of this, they are worthy of our thought and meditation even today. They are true, eternally true, because of Maundy Thursday. The events of that dark and lonely night clearly reflect the truth of the words of our text: "All power is given unto Me in heaven and in earth." These words are evident in our Lord's farewell address, in which He unrolled the carpet of history. They are the undertone of His high-priestly prayer, in which He carried the church of all the tomorrows to His heavenly Father in petition and far vision. They are very real in the first direct contact with His enemies. They become clear in His majestic and powerful silence before those who were killing Him, in all the minutes and hours of that lonely, tragic, and victorious night. Here we see, now more surely than ever before, that the Sign of the Cross, even at its darkest moment, is the sign of power.

It is very easy for the seventieth generation of the men and women after the Cross to lose the vision of its continuing power and victory. We have seen the tremendous contradiction between the faith proclaimed by the church and the faith by which men and women actually live and die in the streets of a mocking world. We see the tremendous odds against which the church of God must fight: the crushing weight of a decaying world, the awful gap between the faith we profess and the faith we live. We know that the things for which we stand and the faith by which we live are today openly hated and despised and cursed just as they were when men and women screamed their hate and defiance of God under a cross nineteen hundred years ago.

There is therefore always the immediate and

imminent danger that our personal lives and the life of the church will be dominated by a crippling spirit of doubt, anxiety, and fear. There are many who feel that there is only weariness in the years before us: the pitiful stirring of burnt-out ashes of fires, the deadly routine of tending altars which the world has forgotten. We live in a world without much hope for a better tomorrow.

Such a spirit of doubt and fear is not Christian. It certainly should not be part of our memory of Maundy Thursday and Good Friday. There is a continuing power about the Cross which towers over the momentary wrecks of time. Everything else may change. The truths by which men attempt to live may sink into chaos and night, the world may grow weary and old, but in the Cross of Jesus Christ is the fountain of eternal power and everlasting youth. The year of our Lord nineteen hundred and fifty-nine is still under the Sign of the Cross — the sign of power!

Although the church seems to be beaten back from one area of human life after another and apparently lives only on the crumbs of men's time and talents, it is nevertheless true that as long as she lives close to the Cross, she is the most powerful phenomenon in the modern world. The Scriptures testify to the fact that the entire period of the New Testament church, which began with the sunrise of Calvary and will end only with the last red sunset of the world, is a day of power and victory. "All power is given unto Me." As members of the church we stand in the long tradition of the day of power against the night of weakness which men have made for themselves. As we sing our hymns and speak our prayers on Maundy Thursday and all other days of the year, we are in line with all the true power of two thousand years. The sudden light over Bethlehem, the Man from Nazareth who spoke words as never yet man spake, the dark hour on Calvary and the glorious hour in the resurrection garden, the long years with their red line of saints and martyrs, the conquering faith of crusader and scholar and reformer — all these testify to the continuing power of the Cross. They lived under the sign of power!

Today we may sometimes feel that the center of power has really finally shifted elsewhere. Surely men no longer live and die for God and Christ and His church. They live by guns and fear and hate. They follow hypnotic voices shouting to the ends of the earth. And yet again and again the continuing power of the Cross demonstrates itself in the lives of men. It is strange how often modern man, pausing for a moment in the madness of life without God, sees the power of the Crucified on the dark horizon of his world. Somehow he seems to know that the figure of the Son of God bearing the sins of the world is the answer to all the problems which trouble and perplex the souls of men. He feels something which he has lost. It is this sense of power which the church in our time must again recover and proclaim to a dying world. We must again be stirred by our Savior's words: "All power is given unto Me." We must be alive to the promise of the Cross, that by its everlasting power it can make, through the forgiveness of sins, our succession of common days a triumphant march to a better world and the high fulfillment of our Cross-given destiny. Seeming defeat will be turned into victory. Human indifference and human bitterness will only cause us to turn from earth to heaven, and our human weaknesses will compel us to turn to the Cross for strength and hope and power.

The life of the world and the individual proceeds by twos. There is an evident duality in life: body and soul, good and evil, light and darkness, night and day. One day this duality will end. There will be only one victory — and it will be ours! Through the shadows of Maundy Thursday and Good Friday, through the darkness of the evening time of the world our eyes must be fixed once more today on the Cross of Jesus Christ, eternally young, eternally strong, and finally eternally victorious. It is the great continuing sign of power!

And now the strange, mysterious thing about

all this is that men must be driven to their knees before they can really see the ultimate meaning of Maundy Thursday and Good Friday. Driven to their knees by the consciousness of their sin, by the breaking down of fellowship with God, they are completely ruined. Sin is bad in the world, worse in the church, and worst of all in the relationship between God and man. Have you ever noticed how every reference in Holy Writ uses this picture? Sin is wandering, loneliness, going away, going astray, separation. There is always the same tolling theme! We have lost the power to make our life strong and full of hope.

On Maundy Thursday and Good Friday we see now the amazing, humanly incredible sign of the power of the Cross. This is the power and miracle of forgiveness, the restoration of fellowship, the return to the Father's house. In our Lord and Savior's suffering on Calvary our brokenness is healed and our union with God and man restored. Our great separation, so long now and so bitter, has been ended by the reunion with God through Jesus Christ. The bonds of sin are loosed. We have again the freedom beneath and beyond all human freedoms: the freedom from fear of sin, the freedom from want of God, the freedom of worship of God, the freedom of speech to God! Maundy Thursday and Good Friday tell us that this is an accomplished fact. We are facing a finished redemption. In our time, too, many men have made an effort to make our faith a quest instead of an achievement! As Christians we must say to them that in contrast to all other religious systems the faith of Christianity is a fact, done and complete, and not a search for higher truth. The essence of Christianity is that something has been done and nothing remains to be done. It is finished — holy, powerful, and perfect!

And how that message fits into our world with its haunting sense of incompleteness, of unfinished faith, of broken dreams and lost hopes. This is our faith: "Only once in the long story of our incompleteness there was one task that was done completely, finally, and absolutely." It remains now as the last continuing sign of power over the world. Our Lord's atonement gives us the power to stand up before God, ladies and gentlemen of His choosing, unashamed and unafraid. This is the heart of our great faith. It is good for us to remember it once more this Maundy Thursday and to live by it — and perhaps to bring it to our world, however haltingly and humbly, so that others, too, might come under the sign of the power of the Cross.

The
SIGN
of
FINALITY

Jesus said, It is finished!   JOHN 19:30

Father, into Thy hands I commend My spirit.
LUKE 23:46

Fifteen hundred years ago St. Anselm ascended his pulpit on Good Friday and said: "I do not know if I wish to speak today. Why should I speak when my Savior is silent and dies?" Certainly every preacher has felt much the same way. All he can really ask his people to do is think quietly and personally about the meaning of the Cross, now that the great drama draws to its close.

Today, therefore, we wish to consider, in Good Friday humility and silence, two sentences at the very close of the scene on Calvary. They are probably the greatest in all the history of human speech. They cover all of life and the shadow of death. The first is: "It is finished!" By this we can live. The second is: "Father, into Thy hands I commend My spirit." By this we can die. To think about these two sentences is therefore a very good way to spend a part of Good Friday.

Let us look at the setting. It is now about three o'clock in the afternoon, the last few moments in the drama of the Cross. The crowd has become a good deal more quiet. Even mobs become still when death rides. Suddenly the head goes up once more under the crown of thorns, and in a loud voice our Lord and Savior says, "It is finished!" The meaning of this sentence must be perfectly clear to all of us. To the Pharisees standing around the cross, to the Roman soldiers, if they had eyes to see and ears to hear, these words must have sounded like the crack of doom. Had they after all lost? They were killing Him, but He seemed to feel that He had won a victory. Yes, if they had eyes to see and ears to hear, they would have seen each thorn in His crown become a shining gem in His diadem of glory. They would have seen the nails forged into the scepter of a king. They would have seen His wounds clothe Him with the purple of empire. He had won a great, final, and eternal victory. The world was changed.

66

Until the end of time history would now be divided into before and after. He had won a victory which was decisive for all men. All men would now have to decide on their attitude over against the Cross. There could be no neutrality. From this moment on He would be either a stone of stumbling or the Way of life and to life.

If we look more closely at our Lord's dying words, "It is finished," we see that He is not referring to the fact that His agony is now ended, that the malice, the hatred, the pain, the heart broken with sorrow are now done and set aside forever. Nor is He merely saluting death as so many brave men have done before and since Good Friday. Nor is He merely saying good-by to life, the years flashing swiftly before His mind, tired of Himself, tired of life, as Hamlet said, "To sleep, perchance to dream" and "The rest is silence." No, it should be perfectly clear that this is the cry of a worker whose work was done, of a soldier whose warfare was ended, of a Savior whose work had been accomplished. We of the twentieth century must be especially sure of this. He has in His grip these days and these years and what we have done to Him and to one another. His is the power and the glory forever and ever.

For proof of this we can, of course, turn to the pages of Holy Writ to find echoes of His final cry. "Wherefore God also hath highly exalted

Him and given Him a name which is above every name, that at the name of Jesus every knee should bow." There are many passages like this. Today, however, we should like to point to another proof which reflects the full meaning of His words, "It is finished." Let us turn for a moment to His enemies, to the indifferent, some of whom are in the churches of Christendom today. They are one of the great testimonies to His continuing power. They simply cannot leave Him alone! His enemies still hate Him. Men do not hate the dead. Hate dies when the object hated dies. No one today hates Napoleon or Genghis Khan. Men no longer clench their fists against a Bismarck or stand guard over the tomb of a Nelson. But they still clench their fists against Christ, and they still stand guard over His tomb. They say He is helpless and dead, but they pour out literature against Him and His church. They build philosophies of government and life constructed to shut Him out. They clench their fists when His very name is mentioned. Why? Men do not fight ghosts. There are two kinds of faith: the saving faith of the redeemed and the protesting faith of the damned, and both of them always testify to the sign of power in Christ and His Cross. We see evidence of His continuing power in the books His enemies write against Him, in their laughter over His church, in their cynicism concerning the power of His Gospel. Day after

68

day, as long as the world stands, His enemies testify to His mysterious hold over men and life and time.

Why? Francis Thompson in "The Hound of Heaven" writes a line which sums it all up. He points clearly to the reason why men still look at Jesus strangely as He passes by in life and in history. For time and eternity it is true, as Thompson says, "All things betray thee who betrayest Me." That's it! All things betray man when he betrays his Lord and Savior Jesus Christ. All the good things in life which He made, love and laughter and sunshine and health, become dust and myrrh and ashes without Him. On Good Friday more men and women know it than on any other day of the year. Perhaps that is the reason for the crowded churches. Once more they feel the strange, mysterious power of His words, "It is finished!"

We who by His grace and pity have made His victory our victory can now live on and on by His cry, "It is finished!" Our sins are now forgiven. Our souls are cleansed. Our consciences are clear and clean. Our incompleteness has ended in His final word. Our unfinished tasks and our broken lives are complete, finished, and made whole by Him who loved us so much that He would rather die than be without us. His cry,

"It is finished," makes it clear that we now, too, can join in His victory.

Every thoughtful man and woman knows that the greatest continuing and haunting sorrow of life is just its sense of incompleteness, of unfinished tasks, of things that we would like to do and cannot do. Life is full of loose ends and frayed edges. Of course, we often say, "This is done and finished," but what we mean to say is, "It is the best I can do just now. Perhaps someday I shall be able to do better." So the end of anything in life is never complete and final. Time and life are much too fluid for that.

Here, however, on the cross we have in the long story of our incompleteness and imperfection one task that was done completely, finally, and absolutely by any standard of measurement, human or divine. The work of our Lord from the first cry in the manger to the last cry on the cross was a divine symphony coming to its final and inevitable end. "It is finished!" And with the finishing of His task our sins are forgiven, and we stand before God in the complete perfection of His atoning life and work.

The second sentence is equally important. "Father, into Thy hands I commend My spirit." Here is something by which we can die. Men have always been interested in the way humanity has met death. Men's dying words are always significant. Macbeth said: "Out, out, brief candle; life's but a walking shadow." Goethe cried: "Light! More Light!" Anatole France said: "Draw the curtain; the farce is played out." Men have faced death in protest or in shrugging acceptance. They have run the entire gamut of emotions when they are face to face with the final and universal fact of life.

There is nothing like that in our Lord's last word. His head goes up once more. He is now facing His heavenly Father alone. The crowd has been forgotten. The pain of the crucifixion is almost in the past. He is coming home now, the long adventure over, carrying in His hands the atonement which He has made for all the sins of the world. In the great halls of heaven cherubim and seraphim wait for Him, the tall lilies of heaven bend left and right, and the choirs of eternity stand silent. He has commended His spirit into the hands of His heavenly Father. We know that all the angels rejoice because the one poor thief with Him is the first of a long procession of men and women who will storm the gates of heaven with His blood covering their sins and His love bringing them home. This is a great and goodly company. By faith in His atoning work we, too, can join them.

We have all seen a mother putting her child to bed. The child protests. It wishes to stay up just a little longer. There are so many things still to be done. And so also we, when the final word comes to us. Toward twilight we hear a voice saying to us: "Now put away your toys, the little things with which you worked in life, the patch-work of your plans and your dreams. It is time for you to say your prayers and go to sleep." We, too, shall ask for just a little more time, a few more hours.

But then something great and wonderful and eternal will happen just as it happened to our Lord on Good Friday. We, too, will commend our spirit into the hands of our heavenly Father. And as for Him, so also for us, there will be another morning — the great morning of God. We shall wake up to see something very splendid and very beautiful. Flaming and glowing on the tapestries of heaven will be all the little things which we began to do and tried to do here on earth, cleansed, glori-fied, and transfigured by Him who has preceded us and who now pleads for us before the throne of His heavenly Father through all eternity. He has finished our little tasks for us. They have been finished by hands that once were torn by nails and that reached out for heaven at the last moment.

There is a great medieval picture of Calvary which tells this story better than mere words. At first glance it is the usual picture of the crowd and the three crosses. But over in the corner there is a man taking off his shoes! There is peace and joy in his face. He is taking off his shoes because here at Calvary he has come home. So in all the churches of Christendom today, all those that stand in the light of the Cross have come home to the home of warmth and love and no loneliness at all. This is the power of the Cross also over the final fact of death.

It remains for us, as another Good Friday comes and goes, to tie all the loose ends together so that they can never break. Down in the gutter of the city street there is a drop of water, stagnant, soiled, and dirty. From far up in the heavens the sun falls upon it, warms it, fills it through and through with its strange new life, lifts it up higher and higher, beyond the clouds. Then one day it falls as a snowflake, white and clean and pure, on a mountaintop. This is the whole story of our life in Christ and with Christ. Our own lives, often so soiled, so tawdry, so low, and so worn, can be lifted on the wings of the morning if we give them to Him who once was lifted up on Good Friday and who commended His spirit into the hands of His heavenly Father. We, too, can be lifted up until we walk the high places of the earth, unashamed and unafraid, living in the company of Him who died that we might have life and have it more abundantly, for His is the kingdom and the power and the glory forever and ever.

And so He goes home now to His Father on that first Good Friday; and, as we watch Him go, what shall we say? Perhaps only the old intimate words:

Your arms are strong around me, and I know
That somehow I shall follow where you go,
To the still land beyond the evening star
Where everlasting hills and valleys are.
And evil shall not hurt me any more,
And terror shall be past, and grief and war.

"Father, into Thy hands I commend My spirit." Certainly there is no better and no greater way to die than that. This is the ultimate, final sign of the finality of the Cross.

The
SIGN
of
HIS PRESENCE

But they constrained Him, saying, Abide with us; for it is toward evening, and the day is far spent. And He went in to tarry with them.

And it came to pass, as He sat at meat with them, He took bread and blessed it and brake and gave to them.

And their eyes were opened, and they knew Him; and He vanished out of their sight.

And they said one to another, Did not our heart burn within us while He talked with us by the way and while He opened to us the Scriptures?

LUKE 24:29-32

Few stories in the entire Sacred Record are more dear to the Christian heart than the story

75

of Emmaus. Here in a few sentences all the comfort and glory of Easter are applied directly to the problems of life and living. Here we see, clearly and finally, the meaning of the open tomb for our own journey toward the last sunset. The entire story is a striking parable of human life. It began in confusion and pain and ended in faith and joy. It began in darkness and ended in the white light of the Sun of Righteousness. It began in loneliness and ended in the magnificent truth that since Easter morning no believing heart need ever be alone again.

The story itself is familiar to Christian memory. On the afternoon of the first Easter Day many years ago, two of the sorrowing disciples, weary with the black memory of Good Friday, were walking toward Emmaus. Their hearts were filled with sadness and fear. They were face to face with the end of everything they had hoped and believed. Three days had come and gone since the news of His death had reached them. Nothing more had happened. True, a few of the faithful women had been at the sepulcher that morning and had astonished them by reporting that the body was not in the grave. That, however, seemed to be only a wild rumor.

As they walked and talked, our Lord joined them on the way. Their eyes, dark with sorrow and blinded with tears, did not recognize Him.

He asked the reason for their sadness. They told Him the story of the mighty words and deeds of Him whom they had now lost, of His shameful death, of the ruin of all their hopes and dreams, and of the strange report of the women on that third morning. Their recital ended with the simple, sorrowing words: "But Him they saw not." No matter what they had heard, they wanted to see Him. If only they could see Him once more! If only they could know that He was alive! Then all that had gone before would be as a momentary dream in the night, lost and forgotten in the light of His presence.

And then the Stranger spoke! "And beginning at Moses and all the prophets, He expounded unto them in all the Scriptures the things concerning Himself." He reached far back into the dawn of time in order to show them why Good Friday and the Cross had to come. He spoke of Moses and David and Isaiah. He showed them how the prophets had foretold everything that had happened. This was no sudden and unexpected event planned and executed by the powers of darkness. All of it, every single step, was a part of the eternal counsels of the Holy Trinity, conceived in eternity and executed in time: "Ought not Christ to have suffered these things and to enter into His glory?" This was the great divine "ought," the eternal "must." All these things ought to be,

He told them, in order that through the glory of Bethlehem, the pain of Good Friday, and the victory of Easter the souls of men might be redeemed.

But still they knew Him not! Only after He had gone in to tarry with them, the simple little act of breaking the bread and blessing it suddenly opened their eyes so that they knew Him. Perhaps their memory suddenly went back to the days when they had seen Him do this in Galilee and Judaea. "Their eyes were opened, and they knew Him." The grave was really empty! Their Lord was alive! He had won the final victory over death. Now they knew that Easter had come.

Many centuries before the still dawn of Easter Day a great cry, wrung from the heart of Job, began to echo across the waiting ages: "I know that my Redeemer liveth." Taken up and repeated by countless saints, in the years of life and the hours of death, it became the great, eternal message of the open grave and the empty tomb. Early in the morning the women hurrying to the grave with the sorrow of death returned from the grave with the joy of life. The stunned silence of the disciples, torn between the warm faith of their hearts and the hard fact of the Cross, became the everlasting antiphon for the voice of Job. "I know that my Redeemer liveth." All the ages could now sing it, and all men could now know it. The stone rolled away had been made by the hand of God a witness to His eternal power and a monument to His living presence.

The story of Emmaus has been repeated countless times since that first Easter evening. By the grace of God it can also be our story. Its courage and victory can come also to us, who live so far down the ways of time. "Abide with us, for it is toward evening, and the day is far spent."

One of the dark marks of our time is its uncertainty. Men are not sure of anything. In fact, it has become fashionable to doubt. It is considered smart and sophisticated to be uncertain. The result has been ruin and death. In such an age nothing is more desperately important than the question: Is there anything that is sure and permanent in life?

The answer lies in our Easter faith. There is nothing vague or mysterious or indefinite about it. Its message is: Christ lives. He lives with us. He lives for us. A believing child can understand this. It is clear and sure. It is a fact witnessed by history and certified by faith.

Just how does He live with us? Although He ascended into heaven on the afternoon of Ascension Day, He did not leave the disciples afraid and alone. Within a few days they became a conquering host. Confounded and appalled by the tragedy of Good Friday, huddled behind locked doors in hidden houses in Jerusalem, they became the indomitable bearers of the Cross, the men and women before whom the Roman Empire began to tremble. If they became living faggots, they knew they were torches of the Gospel. If they died, their faces at the moment of death were like Stephen's, the "face of an angel." They lived "under the long looks of God and His glances of a thousand years." Why? Because He had answered their prayer "Abide with us" with the great sentence which ends all loneliness and fear for the Christian heart: "Lo, I am with you alway, even unto the end of the world." It is true that we cannot see Him with our eyes or touch Him with our hands. He has His own way of being with us in the world. It is a great and a sure way. It stretches beyond and above the noise of the world and the dark highways of men as the great, shining highway of the King of kings. This way lies in His Word and His sacraments. He comes to us through these means of grace. In them and through them He enters our hearts. There is no other way by which we can live in His abiding presence. No good works or seemingly holy life will bring Him to us. At Emmaus the disciples remembered that He had opened the Holy Scriptures to them: "Did not our heart burn within us while He talked with us by the way and while He opened to us the Scriptures?" So He comes to us today through His Word, and our eyes are opened to His presence by His grace. When He ascended from the earth in His glorified body to rule the centuries from the right hand of His Father in heaven, He left us His life, His death, His forgiveness in the pages of the Holy Scriptures and in the sacraments. Through them the story of Emmaus was to be repeated again and again, every day and every hour of Christian history. By them the Comforter was to bring faith into our sorrowing hearts and companionship to our lonely lives. They were to bring us the blessed assurance of the forgiveness of sins, peace, and salvation.

Do not our hearts burn within us as we remember today how often we have neglected these means of His coming into our lives? On the way to Emmaus the eyes of the disciples were darkened by sorrow and fear. Somehow they had to be opened again to the glory and power of His abiding presence. Today, when our hearts are so often shadowed by the darkness of hate and blood, by our countless fears over the future, by the storms of war, dare we neglect the only way in the world by which faith and courage and hope can come alive again in our eyes? This is the way to Emmaus — with Him. Even today it winds past the noise and confusion of the world to the pulpit and altar of our church and to the Bible in our homes. There our Lord waits to answer all our questions and end all our fears.

By the grace of God this can be our first lesson today: Our risen Savior abides with us in His Word and sacraments. When we use them faithfully, regularly, frequently, He draws near to us. Our eyes are opened and we see Him. Our faith beholds Him as He was foretold by prophets, born in the manger, dying on the cross, breaking the tomb, so that He may now abide with us forever, here by the means of grace and there by the vision of glory. This is most certainly true!

Everything our Lord does is done for us. We are the objects of His eternal love. When He comes to us and abides with us, He has certain definite purposes in His mind and heart. He wishes to give us something. His presence means something great and beautiful. The disciples at Emmaus knew that. Their plea "Abide with us" was based on the statement "for it is toward evening, and the day is far spent." It was growing dark. The Stranger who had opened the Scriptures to them would be good company for the coming night. As they had listened to Him, their hearts had burned with a new courage and a far hope. They wanted Him to stay with them because in His presence they had found a new understanding of the counsels of God and their meaning for history and life.

This has always been the blessed experience of the believing heart. The presence of the risen Savior changes everything in life. Absolutely everything! Forty days after Emmaus He was standing with His disciples on a hillside in Galilee. His voice came to them like the rush of mighty waters which would tear them from their moorings and hurl them over the Roman Empire. "Go ye and teach all nations." Because of the magnitude of this task He immediately added the words which repeat the shining story of Emmaus: "Lo, I am with you alway, even unto the end of the world." Although a cloud was about to take Him away from their sight, no cloud and no shadow would ever come between Him and the vision of their faith. If happiness was to come to them, it would be the happiness reflected from the light of His presence; if honor, it was to be the honor of Calvary; if glory, it was to be the glory of His love. He would abide with them forever.

This must be our prayer after these many years. If we ask Him, He always stays.

Countless men and women have lived and died in His presence for almost two thousand years. It is still the best way to live and to die. The entire Holy Scriptures end with the moving words, "Come, Lord Jesus." Whenever and wherever these words are spoken in repentant faith, we hear His answering voice, old and lovely, healing and tender, "Yea, I come quickly." He crosses the threshold of our hearts, and life can never be the same again. In the continuing mercy of His presence we can forget the huge invisible load of care and sin, the intolerable burden of the remembered years, and all the cares and sorrows which make life so dark for the men and women who walk the ways of the world without Him.

This is what His abiding presence can do for us also today. As seldom before in the history of the world, men have lost their faith in man-made things. They have found that education and science cannot give the final answer to the problems which trouble and perplex the souls of men. They are haunted by a feeling of failure and defeat. Also the Christian heart is sometimes touched by this universal feeling of futility and despair. When we look at our own lives, we find that we are seldom completely happy. We are aware of our own weaknesses and defeats. We remember old sins and old troubles. We feel that the world about us is rushing toward destruction. Our weary hearts cry out for the living God, for the calm peace and sure rest which can be found in Him alone. The Easter message of the abiding presence of the risen Savior is the only possible solace and comfort for our ills. It tells us that we can now live with Him who took all our troubles and sins up to Calvary and buried them in the forgiveness of God. It assures us that through the forgiveness of sins we can begin each day anew. As we walk with His nail-torn hands in ours, life begins to move and live. It is no longer a dull routine. We live with Him. He knew its meaning and purpose. The world may say: "Happy is the man who is rich, who is powerful, who is popular, who enjoys life, who can do what he wants to do." Our Savior tells us that the world is fearfully wrong. Across the tears and the graves of those who thought that the world was right He comes into our lives to tell us that with Him there is a new set of standards and an eternal value and importance in our brief journey between the cradle and the grave. In His presence we cannot be afraid, because He is not afraid; we cannot be dismayed, because He is not dismayed; we cannot be conquered, because He will not be conquered. Facing all the storms and tears of life, there is always Someone by our side who knew them all and suffered them all for our sakes.

This is the continuing power and glory of our Easter faith. As the shadows of time lengthen and the hour of man grows late, we shall need this faith more than ever before. Much work remains to be done in the world so that the message of the risen Savior may be brought to new millions sitting in an old darkness. Finally, only the men and women who live in the abiding presence of the King of kings can bring peace and hope to the hurt and bewildered souls of men.

Our Savior's company can never be an excuse for idling and drifting through life. While He gives us peace for our souls, He also gives us work for our hands. Since we live with Him, we have the blessed privilege of bringing Him to others who do not know the grace and power of His presence. Our days and years belong to Him, and He asks us to use them for Him until the night comes. Just as the disciples at Emmaus hurried back to tell others that they had seen their Lord, so we are called to go out into the world of our friends, our neighbors, and our enemies and tell them of His everlasting grace and mercy.

"Abide with us, for it is toward evening, and the day is far spent." Let this be our humble and heartfelt prayer as we again behold the glory of Easter and its meaning for us. Let it be for us the assurance that in the Word and sacraments our Savior is here with us and will never leave us nor forsake us. Let it be for us a challenge to work for Him and with Him while we wait for the day when He will come again to translate our faith in His abiding presence into the vision of His eternal victory.